# BERWICK
## UPON TWEED

Text by M. Scott Weightman BA
Photographs by Jim Walker FRPS

ABOVE: Edward I.

Berwick became prosperous as a result of its advantageous position. Situated on the lowest crossing point of the Tweed, it possessed a natural harbour and was the focal point of the Tweed Valley, noted for wool and fish.

Sited on the border and on the main route between England and Scotland, it was the first place to feel the effects of any war between the two countries. Between 1173 and 1482 Berwick was captured or sacked on fourteen occasions!

When the Scottish King Malcolm won a decisive victory over the English army in 1018, Berwick prospered as part of Scotland and the River Tweed became a Scottish river. Malcolm's reign began the golden age of Berwick which lasted over 250 years until the capture of the town by King Edward I, the Hammer of the Scots, in 1296.

Within this golden age Berwick was one of the first royal burghs to be established by King David I. A castle was built and during the reign of Alexander III of Scotland (1249–86) Berwick reached the height of its prosperity. In 1286 when the total customs revenue of England was about £8,800, Berwick customs amounting to £2,190 were paid annually into the Scottish exchequer. The main exports were wool and hides, while imports included French wine and Flemish cloth.

In 1296 war broke out between England and Scotland. When Alexander III of Scotland died there were no direct heirs to the Scottish throne, and at an assembly in the great hall of Berwick Castle in 1292

Edward I gave Scotland to John Baliol. Soon after, Scotland and France made a treaty to aid each other in the event of a war. This infuriated Edward who invaded Berwick from land and sea.

The naval attack was repelled but the Berwick burghers were taken by surprise and overrun by the English infantry led by Edward, who gave orders that all men of the town, said to be as many as 7,000, should be put to death. The massacre took place on Good Friday, and signalled the end of Berwick's golden age.

Edward I realized the importance of securing a firm base in Berwick and ordered the building of permanent fortifications. It is said that the king himself laid the first stones of the walls, which were mainly constructed during the reign of Edward II and strengthened by Robert the Bruce in 1320. Altogether there were nineteen towers and five gates along the 2½ mile (4km) length of the walls, which reached 22 feet (7m) in height.

In 1306 the Countess of Buchan was captured by the English after crowning Robert the Bruce king of Scotland at Scone. She was taken to Berwick and imprisoned in a wooden cage for four years in one of the turrets of Berwick Castle.

The castle ruins can be seen from the station platform and the White Wall of 1297–8 descends to the river's edge.

From the castle, the best approach to the Edwardian walls is along Northumberland Avenue. Here the Bell Tower still has a medieval base but was rebuilt in the mid 16th century.

As its name suggests, Scotsgate was the main gate on the road to Scotland. The original gate, completed in 1590, was smaller and single arched, in many respects resembling Cowport. At this time it was called New Gate.

In the early 18th century a Main Guard was built nearby in Marygate to house soldiers on duty. It consisted of two rooms, one for officers and the other for lower ranks. Between these rooms was a windowless prison. The Main Guard was used as a guardhouse until 1815 when the 10 p.m. curfew ceased to operate. In that year it was moved to the edge of Palace Green; Scotsgate was rebuilt and widened, and further altered in 1858. From each side of the gate there is access to the ramparts.

Cowport, built in 1595–6, is the only surviving original gateway in the Elizabethan ramparts. The gate is a vaulted tunnel and formerly consisted of an inner wooden door, or portcullis, and an outer wooden door, which was made about 1750 and has recently been restored. The Elizabethan Cowport was approached by a stone bridge over a wet moat.

Cowport is so called because for many centuries cows were pastured outside the walls and brought inside each evening for safety. This practice continued until shortly after the Second World War.

The Shoregate, near the Customs House, leads to the quay. It was rebuilt in the 1760s as a segmental arch. It is sometimes known as Sandgate because in the 16th century, when there was no quay, the way led through Shoregate to the sandy river bank. The gate, earlier known as Fish Port or Fish Gate, still possesses its original wooden doors.

Up the steps from Shoregate, and a short way along Quay Walls, can be found the Custom House. Completed towards the end of the 18th century, it was at first used as a private residence, then as a dispensary from 1826 to 1872.

The fifth and most recent insertion into the Edwardian walls, Nessgate was built in 1815 to provide access to the new pier, and at that time it was also known as Pier Gate. The pier was started in 1810 and took 11 years to complete. It replaced

ABOVE: Cowport. Formerly, the land outside the nearby walls was used for pasturing livestock but today bowls, golf and soccer are played there.

RIGHT: Shoregate gives access from the lower town to the river and the chandlery, which now houses artists and craftsmen.

FAR RIGHT: Scotsgate formerly guarded the main A1 road between London and Edinburgh. Here runners in Berwick's annual 'Round the Walls' race cross the gate.

LEFT: An excellent example of Georgian architecture, the Custom House, which overlooks Quay Walls, was a dispensary from 1826 to 1872.

BELOW: Nessgate, the newest gate of Berwick, is sometimes called Pier Gate, for it allows the visitor to walk along the pier, completed in 1816.

the ruined Queen Elizabeth's pier of 1577. In 1826 a small lighthouse was erected at the end of the pier.

Bridge Gate was found at the north end of the Old Bridge until 1825. It consisted of an archway also known as English Gate. According to Fuller in his *History of Berwick Upon Tweed* (1799), Bridge Gate, 'together with the adjoining guard house, shut up the bridge at its northern extremity. Towards the middle of it are two strong wooden barriers . . . which give additional security to this mode of defence.'

In the 16th century it was artillery, not arrows, that dominated warfare and in January 1558 an eminent English military engineer, Sir Richard Lee, was ordered by Queen Mary to improve Berwick's defences.

While the walls were begun in Mary's reign (1553–8), most of the work was completed in the reign of Elizabeth I (1558–1603). On her accession, skirmishing between English soldiers and the Borderers became a regular occurrence. The Protestant Elizabeth was alarmed at the marriage of Mary Queen of Scots to the French Dauphin since she feared a conspiracy of France, Spain and Scotland against England. She therefore fortified her major Border town against a possible invasion by her Catholic enemies.

The Elizabethan ramparts were built within the Edwardian walls and took over 20 years to complete, but were in a defensible condition by 1565. The project incurred an expenditure of £128,648 between 1558 and 1570, the costliest undertaking of Elizabeth's reign.

When the Elizabethan ramparts were built, they represented the most advanced system of defensive military technology. This included the use of massive projecting bastions, like blunt arrowheads, built of stone and filled with earth. Guns could be placed on the platforms, or cavaliers, which allowed an all round field of fire towards the prospective invader.

Two bastions are particularly interesting. Meg's Mount, to the west of Scotsgate, was named after the gun which was placed here. A short climb to the cavalier enables a visitor to have magnificent views towards the Cheviots, the Eildons and Halidon Hill.

In the north-east corner of the Elizabethan ramparts stands the Brass Bastion, named from a brass cannon that was mounted on it. From the top of the high cavalier there are superb sea views and most of the walls and fortifications can be

ABOVE LEFT: The walls near Nessgate.

LEFT: Theatre performed against the magnificent backdrop of the Elizabethan walls. Throughout the year, the Maltings Arts Centre promotes a splendid programme of entertainment to suit every taste.

BELOW: Flankers were areas between the main wall and the arrowhead of the bastion. To protect the main or curtain wall, guns were fired through tapering slits known as embrasures. A tunnel led from here, through the ramparts, to the town.

seen from here. One unique feature of the Brass Bastion is the sentry path, a cobbled walk which formerly ran the length of the Elizabethan ramparts.

Between the two is Cumberland Bastion, originally called Middle Bastion but renamed after the Duke of Cumberland, the victor of Culloden in 1746.

At the southernmost point of the ramparts is Coxon's Tower, used as a lookout but with a sloping parapet to allow defenders to fire downwards at the enemy. Improvements to the walls were carried out 1639–53 when an earthwork parapet covered the sentry wall and the cavaliers were raised on all the bastions.

Minor changes were made to the walls after the Jacobite rising of 1745–6, but they have remained virtually unchanged in the years since then.

ABOVE: The arrowhead of the Windmill Bastion has 19th-century gun mountings on its cavalier (or platform).

RIGHT: The Civil War Society re-enacts the assaulting of Berwick's Elizabethan walls. Pageants, tattoos and other outdoor events are a regular feature of the summer scene.

It is believed that the present Old Bridge was the fifth to span the Tweed. The first was swept away in a flood in 1199 and the second destroyed by King John in 1216. Another great flood destroyed the third in 1294 and for 200 years there was no bridge at Berwick, the river being crossed by ferry or fords. Henry VII is said to have ordered the building of a wooden bridge at Berwick but it needed frequent repair because of damage by strong currents and ice floes.

When James VI of Scotland travelled south in 1603 to be crowned James I of Great Britain, he found crossing the Tweed hazardous and is reputed to have said, 'Is there ne'er a man in Berwick whae can work stanes to make a brig over the Tweed?'

In 1611 exchequer funds were made available and the present bridge was started. Work went slowly and only in 1624 could the bridge be used. In 1634 it was completed at a cost of £16,000.

The best description of the Old Bridge is to be found in Fuller's *History of Berwick* (1799): 'This beautiful bridge is situated close to the quay . . . 60 yards below the site of the old timber bridge. It is built of fine hewn stone and has fifteen spacious and elegant arches. It measures 1,164 feet (360m) in length, including the land stalls. Its width is 17 feet (5m). At each of the pillars which are fourteen in number there is an outlet to both sides; without these there would be much greater danger in walking or riding along the bridge than there is at present.'

MAIN PICTURE: The Royal Border Bridge, 2,152 feet (662m) long, has 28 arches each with a span of 61 feet (19m). It reaches a height of 126 feet (39m) above the river bed. The Edwardian walls can be seen on the left.

The Royal Border Bridge is one of the finest railway viaducts in the world. It was designed by Robert Stephenson and built 1847–50. The resident engineer was George Bruce, who was only 25 years old but was destined to become one of the most famous Victorian railway engineers.

Over 2,000 men worked on the project, which cost £253,000 and was opened by Queen Victoria and Prince Albert on 29 August 1850.

ABOVE: The engineer Robert Stephenson.

New Bridge stands between Old Bridge and the Royal Border Bridge. During the first quarter of this century traffic congestion on the A1 through Berwick became a major problem. To alleviate this a new concrete road bridge was built between 1925 and 1928, comprising four arches whose spans vary from 167 feet (51m) to 361 feet (110m). It was opened by the Prince of Wales, later Edward VIII, in 1928 and cost £180,000.

RIGHT: The Old Bridge was completed in 1634. Its tallest arch is off-centre, in line with the deep-water channel.

Holy Trinity Church was built with the stone from Berwick Castle. It stands on the spot where David Bruce married Joan, daughter of Edward II. It was from here that John Knox began his ministry in 1549. A gifted and fiery preacher, he played a vital role in religious reform and the spread of Puritanism.

Holy Trinity is one of the only two parish churches built during the Commonwealth under Cromwell. Designed by John Young of Blackfriars and completed between 1650 and 1652, the church is Puritan in design. Rectangular in shape, when first built it lacked altar, steeple, bells, chancel, stained glass, a font and an organ.

Since that time, the parish church has acquired all three features associated with divine worship. In 1855 the chancel was built and 16th and 17th-century Flemish glass was used in the west window. The bells for divine service were for many years rung from the Guildhall, but in 1951 a service bell was hung in Holy Trinity.

The Guildhall (or Town Hall) dominates the centre of the town. Its 150 feet (46m) spire can be seen from most points along the walls.

Work was begun in 1750 and almost completed by 1754. The architects were Samuel and John Worrall, although a local carpenter, Joseph Dods, claimed credit for the design as he slightly modified the Worralls' original plans. A century ago not only did the council meet here but the police station, courts and gaol were all housed in the building.

In appearance the building is strongly reminiscent of a Classical church and on many occasions has been mistaken for the parish church. The belfry of the Guildhall houses eight bells, including the one formerly rung for church services.

BELOW: A roundel from Holy Trinity Church showing one version of Berwick's coat of arms.

ABOVE: John Knox.

RIGHT: The parish church was built near the site of a 12th-century medieval church, also called Holy Trinity. During the reign of Edward VI, John Knox preached here to soldiers and townsfolk.

**ABOVE:** A local early 19th-century banknote for one guinea (£1.05).

**RIGHT:** The floodlit portico of the Guildhall.

**BELOW:** Visitors to the Guildhall are often allowed to try their hands at bellringing. The bells originate from 1754. The curfew bell still rings at 8 p.m. when all good citizens should be putting out their fires and going to bed!

In the 17th century it was the custom throughout the land for soldiers to be billeted in inns and private houses. There were frequent complaints about this in Berwick. In 1705 the mayor appealed to the town's two MPs to use their influence to have a barracks erected in the town. This would be the first to be built in Britain, but it was not until 1717 that work was started. The project took four years to complete because of insufficient funds. Local residents raised the outstanding amount, thankful to be rid of the soldiers!

Berwick Castle was used as a quarry for building stone and these materials were supplemented by bricks made from Tweedmouth clay.

The finished building accommodated 36 officers and 600 men. Originally it consisted of two three-storey blocks facing each other and was approached through an arched gateway. The Clock Block was added in 1739 and the barracks were remodelled in 1799. By 1817 further additions allowed 700 men to be housed.

At the beginning of the 19th century Berwick ceased to be a garrison town but after that the barracks were occupied by the Northumberland Fusiliers (1879–81) and latterly the King's Own Scottish Borderers (1881–1964).

The KOSB Regimental Museum relates the proud story of the Borderer from the Battle of Killiecrankie (1689) to the Gulf War of 1991. Uniforms, equipment, pictures, models and colours are displayed, as well as the jacket worn by Lord Haig when he was Colonel-in-Chief of the regiment.

'By Beat of Drum' is an English Heritage exhibition that chronicles the changing life of the British infantryman from the 16th to the 19th century. Reconstructed scenes include a barrack room (1757) and an army school room (1862).

The Berwick Borough Museum and Art Gallery is housed in the Clock Block. Here you can peer through the 'Window on Berwick', a flashback to yesteryear or, through the mouth of a dragon, enter a Cairo Bazaar to see some fine exhibits donated by shipping magnate Sir William Burrell. A changing programme of exhibitions caters for all ages and tastes.

ABOVE: The Berwick Borough Museum is now housed in the former barracks, visible here in the foreground.

LEFT: An exciting corner of the Berwick Museum, a must for any visitor to the town. It houses a changing programme of exhibitions, which aim to strike an unconventional note, break down barriers and bend the rules.

RIGHT: A tableau from the 'By Beat of Drum' exhibition, showing an army schoolroom of 1862. The exhibition, run by English Heritage, outlines a soldier's life over a 300-year period.

The Wine and Spirit Museum is located in Palace Green and is housed in an old brewery. It displays a collection of brewing artefacts dating from the 18th century. Other buildings house a recreated chemist shop and pottery.

The museum of local and civic history is in the Guildhall. It is open between Easter and September. This was the old town gaol and from the flat roof where prisoners exercised there are wonderful views towards Bamburgh and Holy Island. At the end of the guided tours, visitors are usually permitted to ring the bells.

RIGHT: A reconstructed chemist's shop in the Wine and Spirit Museum. This belongs to the Lindisfarne Liqueur Company and is housed in the Governor's House in Palace Green.

BELOW: The beautiful mute swans are permanent residents of the town and number over 600.

RIGHT: Windsurfing, sailing and rowing are popular summer activities at the river mouth.

BELOW: A 1913 poster extolling the benefits of a holiday in Berwick.

ABOVE: From Quay Walls the narrow medieval passageway, Sallyport, leads to Bridge Street.

LEFT: Shoe Lane, off Bridge Street, leads to the Maltings Arts Centre. The lane was the site of an old shoe factory which has been converted to modern flats. As a reminder of the lane's past, an old shoe-making machine has been used as a decorative feature.

BELOW: Fishing is still carried on but gone are the days when 700 fish could be caught in one day. Hand over hand the net is drawn in to trap the salmon, which have been caught here for over 1,000 years.

For centuries salmon fishing was the most important commercial activity of Berwick. In the 14th century Tweed fisheries were famous. The land on the north side of the river belonged to the Crown and was known as 'Royal Land', the King's Fisheries; the land to the south was known as the Bishop's Fisheries.

In the 16th century there were twelve fisheries on the river. One barrel in twelve of the fish caught was paid as a royalty to Queen Elizabeth I.

At this time salmon fishing was controlled by the town's merchant guilds. The season stretched from February to September and fishing was allowed between sunrise and sunset. Only guild members could rent a fishery, salt and export the fish. Fisheries changed hands for large amounts of money. In 1635 the Moore brothers bought the Bishop's Fisheries for £3,900 and soon after paid £2,900 for the King's Fisheries.

From 1788, the use of ice changed the industry and, with the advent of the railway, salmon could be sent 'fresh' to any part of the country. Between 1808 and 1835 business boomed with record catches. This overfishing led to the Tweed Acts of 1857 and 1859 which restricted the type of nets used and extended the close season.

Today salmon are less plentiful. The book *A Wake for the Salmon* by Jim Walker vividly captures in photographs the men at work in the industry over recent years.

In the 13th century Tweedmouth, on the south side of the Tweed, was a small fishing village facing the more prosperous Berwick on the north bank. Until the 15th century it was used by the English as a base of operations in their conflicts with the Scots. Under King John a castle, twice destroyed by the Scots, was built to fortify the south bank.

Near the Border Bridge 'Hang a Dyke Neuk' is the site where Edward II is said to have executed Sir Alexander Seton's son, a hostage, before the battle of Halidon Hill in 1333.

Tweedmouth parish church boasts a weather vane in the form of a salmon and in the churchyard James Stuart (Jimmy Strength) is buried. He was 115 years of age when he died in 1844. Although many stories are apocryphal, he is said to have carried for a short distance a cart loaded with hay and weighing 1.5 tonnes.

Spittal, further along the riverside, takes its name from the medieval hospital of St Bartholomew, which cared for lepers between 1234 and 1535. In the centuries

that followed, it was famous for smuggling but until recent times fishing and fish processing have always been the most important economic activity.

In the 19th century, industries such as gas chemicals, iron and spade manufacture grew up. Visitors came to the Spa Well, whose waters were reputed to have medicinal qualities. Today the long sandy beach attracts visitors.

ABOVE: Spittal beach. The lighthouse was erected at the end of Berwick Pier in 1826.

BELOW: The silhouette of old gas, chemical and iron works at Spittal is evidence of the town's industrial past.

# The Walled Town of Berwick

**Legend**

| | |
|---|---|
| Route of Walk | |
| Museum | |
| Historic Building | |
| *i* | Tourist Information Centre |
| P | Car Park |
| → | One Way Street |
| M W | Public Toilets |

**BRASS BASTION** ③

**CUMBERLAND BASTION** ②

WALLACE GREEN

Holy Trinity Church

M W *i* P
Start of Walk

**COWPORT**
④

THE PARADE

**KOSB Regimental Museum**

**SCOTSGATE** ①

CASTLEGATE

COXONS LANE

WALKERGATE LANE

CHURCH STREET

**BARRACKS**

'By Beat of Drum' (English Heritage)

**MEG'S MOUNT** ⑨

M W
Bus Station

Berwick Museum

**WINDMILL BASTION** ⑤

GOLDEN SQUARE

MARYGATE

WEST STREET

BANKHILL

**GUILDHALL**

Cell Block Museum P

WOOL MARKET

M W

The Magazine

Lions House

ROYAL TWEED (NEW) BRIDGE

RAVENSDOWNE

Site of Bridge Gate

BRIDGE STREET

HIDE HILL

Maltings Arts Centre

Kings Arms Hotel

SILVER STREET

NESS STREET

**KING'S MOUNT** ⑥

PIER RD

BERWICK (OLD) BRIDGE

SANDGATE

Swimming Pool

PALACE STREET EAST

**NESS GATE**

R I V E R   T W E E D

P
Chandlery

**SHOREGATE**

P
Custom House

PALACE

Wine & Spirit Museum

**FISHERS FORT** ⑦

**QUAY WALLS** ⑧

Main Guard

PALACE GREEN

WELLINGTON TERR

Coxon's Tower

Metres
100   50   0

Yards
50